**Past the world of fiery dragons.**

**Past the dinosaurs.**

CW01597475

**What are you doing Yasmin?**

**The time machine is out of control!**

**Help William...Quickly...HELP**

**The ground is ripped apart.**

**Rocks are flying through the air.**

**Fire is spewing everywhere.**

# Keep it still William........Look!

The speedometer reading is : 200,000,000
two hundred millions years.

## No sign of people.
## How do you stop this thing?

The onboard computer says - Heaton.
What a fantastic place.

It's all white and covered with ice.
We're slowing down.

**Speedo reading 10,000 years and falling.**

Trees and more trees but no sign of people.

Wait a minute. What is that, Katherine?

Only some deer.

No, no - there.
Look!
In the bushes.

Yes, you're right.
There's a group of them.
Hunters I think? Aren't they hairy?

**This machine has gone crackers again!**

**I thought you had fixed it , Elizabeth.**
**Try again.**

**8,000...5,000...3,000...1,500...500**

**We're crossing the BC/AD line.**

**That's better - reading AD 200**

That's amazing. There are hundreds of them.
Hundreds of Roman soldiers on the march
Look at the top of the hill.

**The time chart reads Hadrian's Wall.**
**Location reading - Shields Road, Byker.**

Here we go again. Keep it steady, Yasmin.
Time chart reading - Saxons, Vikings, Normans.
**Location reading: Adam of Jesmond's House.**

What a great place , shouted Elizabeth.
Look at his coat of arms.
Wow - he's a knight!
Seems an interesting guy said Katherine.

Data bank records:
Great friend of the king.
Got himself killed in the Holy Lands.

That's better, Yasmin. We're slowing down now!

**1,600...1,660...1,700...1,735...1745!**

**Heaton Hall belonging to Squire Ridley**

**Massive Pumping Engines**

**Computer data base records:**

**Largest collection of steam engines on planet earth used for pumping water from Heaton Banks Colliery, one of the largest coal mines in the world.**

## Location chart reads Heaton

An estate of seven farmsteads and a large area of open moorland in the north. Population about 150.

Most people live in the village near Heaton Hall the home of Squire Ridley.

# Internet Map Available

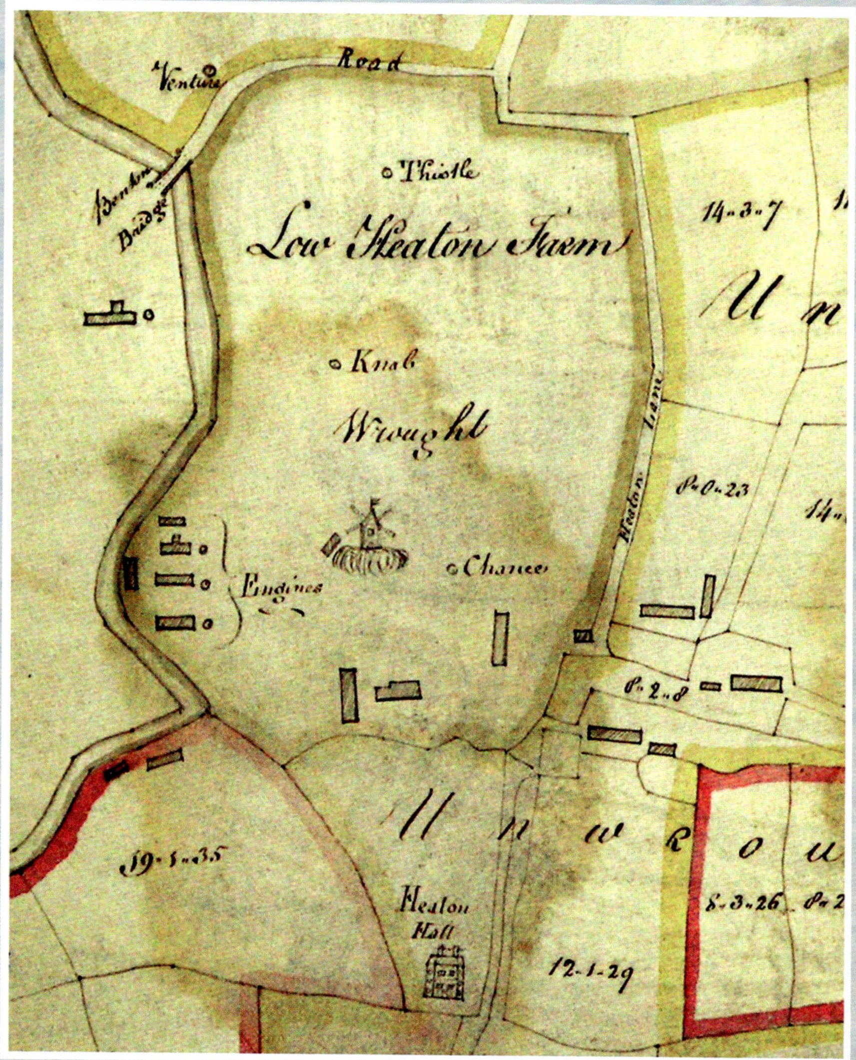


**Old map of Heaton Village
showing the windmill, coal pits and engines
Estimated date 1745**

# Flight Control Panel View
# Location Tyneside - Year 1801

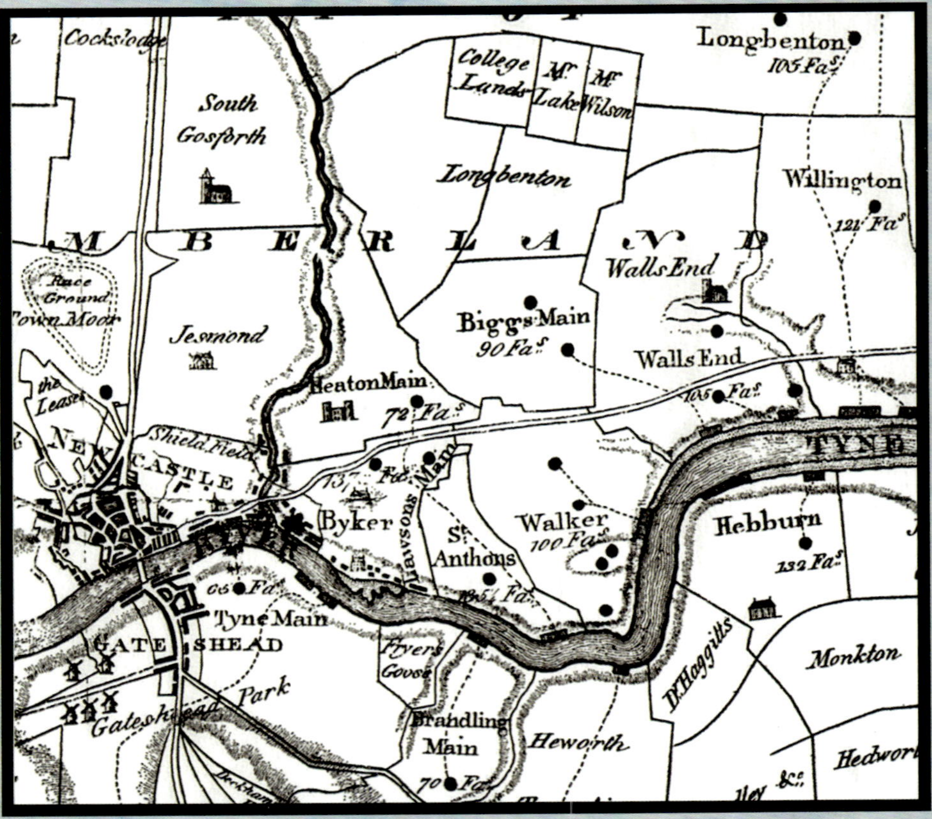


Can you hold her steady, William?
No, no, no - she's off again.
Try harder --- harder --- that's better.
She's stopping now.
Good --- but why is it so dark outside?

## Quick ... Check the Charts

**Location Chart:**

*Heaton Main Colliery*
*High Main Coal Seam*
*342 feet below the surface*

**Time Chart:**

*Year: 1815*
*Day: Wednesday 3rd May*
*Time: 0300 hours*

**Computer Data Base:**

1. One of the largest collieries in the world.
2. Fitted with the latest pumping machinery to remove water from the mine.
3. A railway takes the coal to the River Tyne where it is sent by ship to London and sold to the people to burn in their homes.
4. Over 400 men and boys work at the mine. They are well paid and the mining families earn more money than other workers.
5. No women and no girls are employed at the colliery.

**OUTBOARD CAMERA IMAGE**
**COMPUTER GRAPHICS INTERPRETATION**
**PLAN OF THE COAL MINE**

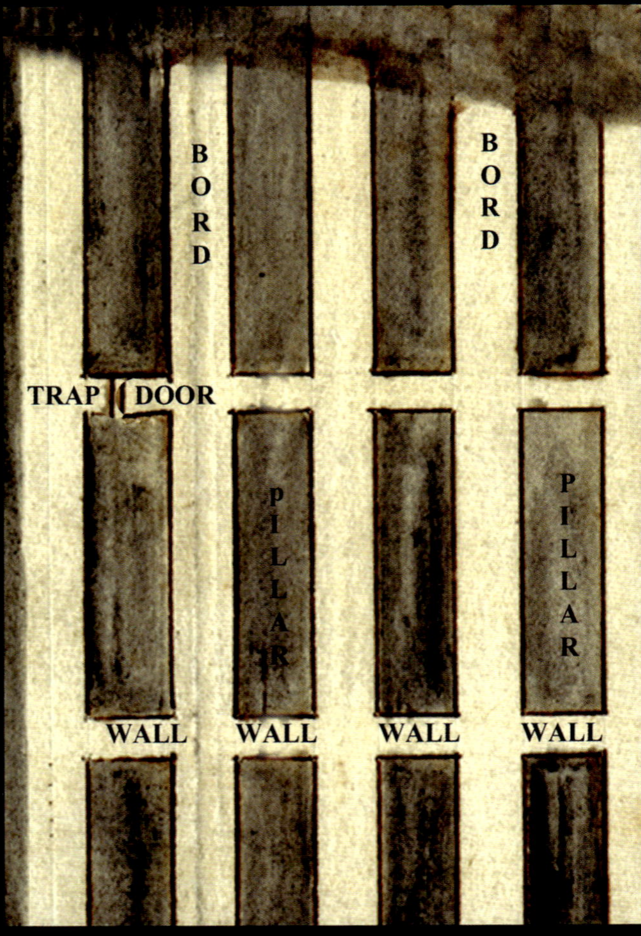


**Bords where the men work**
**Pillars to support the roof**
**Trap door to help with ventilation**
**Walls to divide the pillars**

# Wow - we're underground in a coalmine. This is a plan of the workings.

## Computer Data Base Record

1. Coal is a fossil fuel formed from dead plants decaying in swamps over 300 million years ago. Fossils of leaves, ferns and even trees are found in the coal mines.

2. Coal is a sedimentary rock which is found in beds known as seams. These are between a few inches and many feet thick. The most important seam on Tyneside is called the High Main which is six feet thick in Heaton.

3. Most of the coal is burnt on open fires in people's homes.

4. The smaller coal is used to boil sea water in large pans. The water evaporates leaving salt in the pan.

5. Coal can be heated in ovens to produce coal gas which is used for street lighting.

# Great !

**There are people around.**
**Let's make contact.**

**The database says they speak a strange language - a bit like English but it's called Geordie.**

**Katherine, Yasmin, William and Elizabeth soon made friends with one of the boys - John. He was aged 10 and worked as a trapper boy.**

**He agreed to show them around the mine. William was OK but the girls had to put caps on and pretend to be a boy since girls weren't allowed underground.**

**They took a candle and followed John.**

## What an amazing place !!!

Meet the boys who work in the pit

Tom
Age 7

Tom is a trapper boy. He sits for twelve hours each day opening and closing his trap door to keep the air flowing in the pit. He has a tin lamp for company.

Bill
Age 15

With his pony Lucky Bill moves the coal along the railway to the shaft.

Nick
Aged 15

Nick is a putter.
His job is to push the tubs - it's a hard job!

The most important men are the hewers who use a pick to force the coal down from the coal seam. George Davison cuts the coal by the light of a candle. It is hard work but the pay is very good.

However, the work is very dangerous. Men and boys are killed by falling rocks, exploding gasses and water flooding into the mine.

## The Disaster at Felling in 1812

Candles are risky underground because of the explosive gases. In 1812, there was an explosion at Felling Colliery which killed 92 miners. Several learned men are trying to make a safety lamp. The manager at Heaton Colliery, John Buddle, has been working with the scientist, Humphry Davy. Also, George Stephenson has been making experiments at Killingworth Colliery.

Our fathers take us down the pit when we are about six  years old. No school for us. Well, sometimes we go to Sunday school. William and the girls then showed John the time capsule.    -   **He was amazed!**

They took a brief ride to yesterday and saw the pit by daylight. One big chimney was for the pumping engine which sucked water out or the mine. The other big chimney was for the winding engine which hauled the coal and the miners out of  the mine.

They followed the waggonway to the river where there was a huge staith for loading the coal onto the ships. The waggons carry two and a half tons and are pulled by horses. John taught his new friends a song about the waggonway which was sung in Geordie.

Clap hands for daddy coming
Doon the waggonway
With a pocket full of pennies
And a poke full of hay

The staith was a large wooden building at the riverside. The keel boats collect the coal and ferry it downstream to the collier ships.

There is song we sing about the keelmen.

As I came thro' Sandgate
Thro' Sandgate, thro' Sandgate
As I came thro' Sandgate
I heard the lassies sing.

We'll may the keel row,
The keel row, the keel row
We'll may the keel row
That my laddy's in.

That was all John could remember.

On the way back the explorers visited the pit village where the women were at work. Can you guess what they are doing?

Elizabeth thought that washing day seemed hard work. There were no electric washing machines in 1815. She wondered how the women dried their clothes.

They returned to the pit. It was four o'clock in the morning and the early shift of men and boys were hard at work. John took the four adventurers deeper into the mine.
It was very dark, very wet and very warm.

Suddenly, Willy McCoy, the putter boy appeared shouting .....get out...get out...

**The water's bursting in......**

**Come on said John.**

**We must dash to the shaft.**

## But the shaft is a mile away!

**No, said Yasmin, it's quicker to go to the time capsule.**

**Did you know that the time capsule changes shape to fit the place where it has landed???**

From the onboard camera the adventurers were able to see hundreds of gallons of water pouring down through the mine to the shaft. The water carried everything in its path with it - boys, men, horses, wood, everything.

Some of the miners were able to escape, some were killed immediately,

**but most were trapped in the upper part of the mine..... awaiting rescue!!!**

The adventurers left the time capsule and rushed to the old crane where the trapped miners had gathered. The men had been able to save two of the fifty horses that had worked down the mine.

The boys were really scared. But some of the men had been trapped before and they knew that their friends would be making every effort to rescue them.

All they had to do was wait.... and wait.... and wait. Some prayed for help to arrive soon.

Above ground, the rescue team was very busy. At first, the colliery manager, John Buddle, tried to reach the trapped miners from the Chance Pit. This was an old pit near the windmill in Heaton village. But just as they were making progress sadly the shaft collapsed and filled with sand. Thursday passed ..........

but there was still no sign of the rescuers. By Friday their food was almost gone and by evening time they were very hungry.

**On Saturday they decided to kill a horse!**

Meanwhile, John Buddle was trying to find another old pit in Byker Colliery to restart the rescue. This map shows the old pits on the north side of Shields Road.

Eventually he found the Avenue Pit in the field called Avenue Close. On Friday the rescuers began clearing away the rubbish in the old shaft. The Avenue Pit was about half a mile from the trapped men. Progress was very slow.

**Some thought they could hear noises.**
Some men sang. Some prayed.
Some just lay down to die.
They waited....and waited.....and waited.

On Saturday there was a mighty rush of air as the rescue team broke into the old mine. All the air was drawn from the part of the mine where the men and boys were trapped. Men and boys began coughing.

**Now we are being suffocated!!**

Time to get out of here, shouted William. To the time capsule everyone quickly. But their companion, John, refused to leave his friends.

**That was the last the adventurers saw of their new friend, John the trapper boy.**

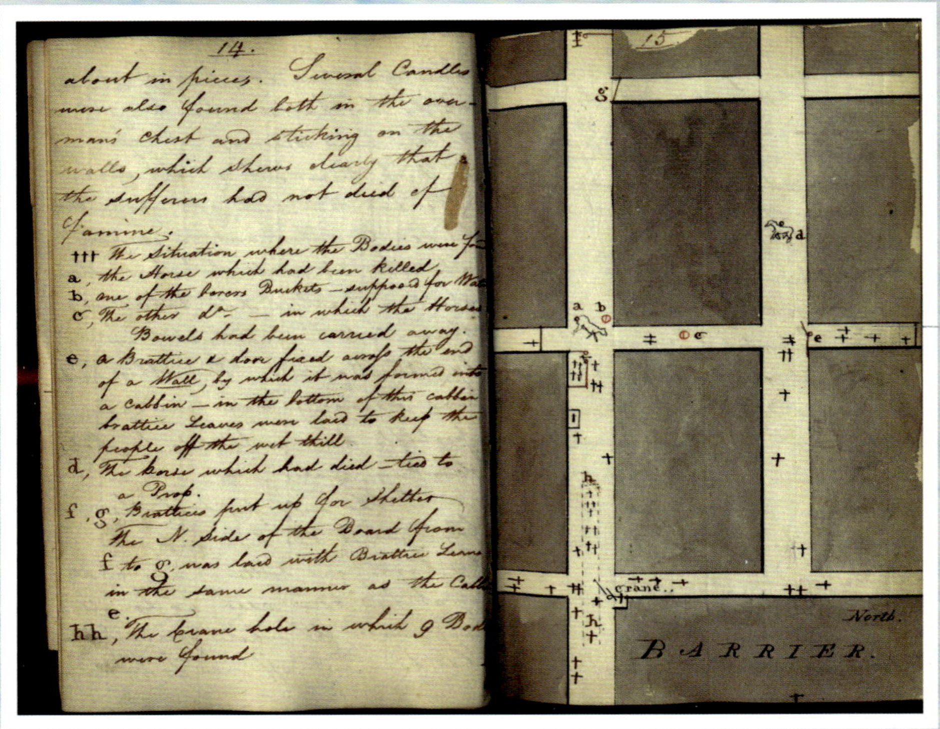
14.

about in pieces. Several Candles were also found both in the over-man's Chest and sticking on the walls, which shews clearly that the sufferers had not died of Famine.

††† The Situation where the Bodies were fo

a, the Horse which had been killed,

b, one of the Corves Buckets — supposed for Wa

c, The other do — in which the Horses Bowels had been carried away.

e, a Brattice & door fixed across the end of a Wall, by which it was formed into a Cabbin — in the bottom of this cabbin brattice Leaves were laid to keep the people off the wet thill.

d, The horse which had died — tied to a Prop.

f, g, Brattices put up for Shelter

The N. Side of the Board from f to g was laid with Brattice Leaves in the same manner as the Cab

hh, The Crane hole in which 9 Bod were found



The time travellers moved on nine months to Wednesday 14th Febraury 1816.

At last the pumps had cleared the water and the rescuers were able to get into the mine. What a strange and sad sight met them. Fifty five bodies lay around the old crane.

These are two pages from John Buddle's notebook. The diagram shows where the bodies of the men and boys were found. Two horses are also marked.

John Buddle led the rescue operations. Notice that he is holding a Davy lamp, which had been invented in autumn 1815. Heaton Main was one of the first collieries to have Davy lamps, which were used by the men trying to rescue the trapped miners.

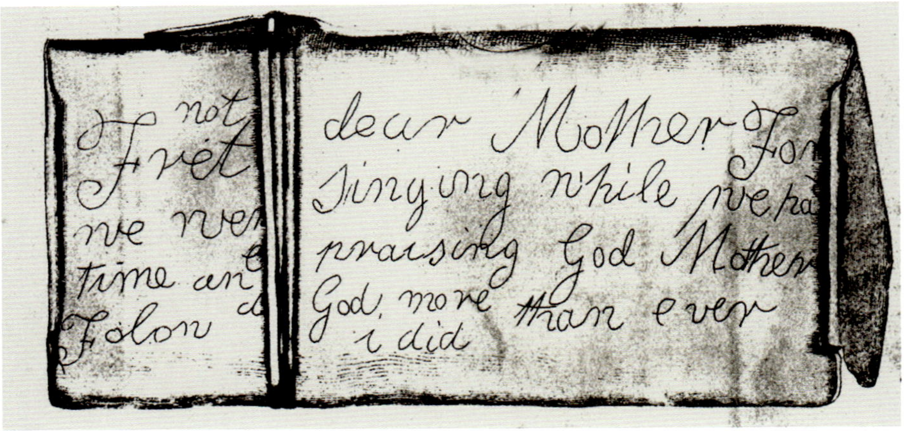


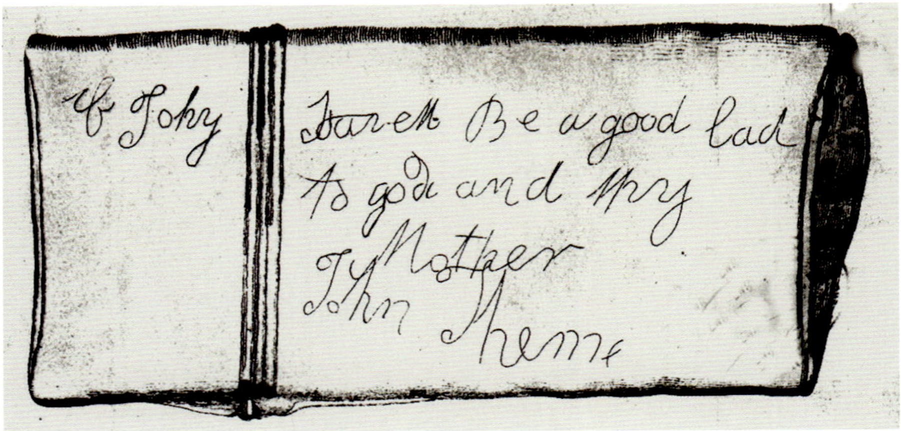


The manager, John Buddle, invited some of the relatives underground to look for the the missing members of their families. One lady, Mrs.Thew, was looking for her husband John and two of her sons, George and Willliam. Mrs. Thew recognised William by his auburn hair and found his candle box in one of his his pockets with a message scatched on it.

The message read - ‘Fret not dear Mother for we were singing while we had time and praising God. Mother follow God more than I ever did’. On the other side was a message from her husband - ‘If Johy be saved be a good lad to god and thy Mother’.

This scene made Elizabeth, Katherine, William and Yasmin very sad. Without her husband’s wages Mrs. Thew, like the other women whose husbands had been killed, had no money to live on. They had to rely on gifts from the local charities.

So ended their adventure beneath the earth. It was exciting to see the great mine and the powerful steam engines pumping water. But the accident showed the risks men and boys had to take to win the coal from the mine. They returned to the time capsule and left for another time and place.

## Every Picture Tells a Story

Look carefully at the sketches on the next two pages. They were drawn by a local artist called Ralph Hedley who was interested in the lives of the miners. They show two very different scenes and tell two very different stories about the miners.

Picture one above is about pay day. This took place on Saturday at the colliery office.

The men are waiting in a line to receive their pay. What are the man and the little girl doing? Do you notice anything odd about them? Can you suggest any reasons why they should be standing there?

Picture two is about Sunday afternoon at the local pub in the mining village. What does this picture tell us about the miners? However, this was not the full story. The Methodist Church was very much opposed to alcohol and was very active within the mining villages.

## Listen to their stories

In 1841 officials from the government visited Heaton Colliery to talk to the boys working in the mine. They wanted to know about the daily life of the boys for a report about children's work which they were writing for Parliament. Here are the stories of two of the boys they interviewed.

**Joshua Stephenson,** aged about eight years, lived in a thatched cottage near Benton. He went down the Middle Pit before he was six years old as a trapper boy. He gets out of bed at 4 o'clock in the morning. The pit finishes at 4 in the afternoon and he gets home about 5 o'clock.

Then he washes himself and gets his dinner, meat and potatoes. After dinner he goes to bed almost directly; he never plays about first.

Goes down the pit in a cage. Takes his bait down with him, mostly bread and cheese, sometimes beef, always as much as he wants.

Some of the boys bray him but not to hurt him. Cannot read at all. Never was at school in his life.

**George Beresford** was almost thirteen. He has been down Benton Pit for four and a half years. Kept a door a bit, then went cleaning the way, then went to driving.

He gets up at half past two every morning because he lives a good way off at Ouseburn which is two or three miles off. Gets to the pit and goes down at 4 o'clock. Drives all day. Goes home to Ouseburn at about 5 o'clock.

Then he gets his dinner, potatoes and meat, then washes himself after dinner and then goes to bed directly, perhaps about 7 or 8 o'clock. Never has time for play.

**THINK**

**Then talk about how the lives of these boys are different from your lives.**

Past the east end of the Central Station and opposite the statue of George Stephenson are two buildings which are very important for this story. One is the Mining Institute where the records of some of the region's famous engineers, such as John Buddle, are kept. Many of these records have been used to write this book. Next door is the home of Newcastle's famous Literary and Philosophical Society where John Buddle and many other mining engineers met to discuss issues of the day such as safety. One of the early safety lamps of George Stephenson is on display. You can visit both of these places of interest.

Charles Hutton
born 1737
died 1823

The son
of a miner
who became one
of Newcastle's
most famous
citizens.

His statue is in
the Lit  and Phil.

Charles Hutton's father and his brothers were miners at Longbenton Colliery and for a time the family lived in High Heaton. Charles was injured in the pit and was sent to school,where he excelled in reading and mathematics. Eventually, he became a renowned teacher of mathematics and one of the most outstanding mathematicians of the eighteenth century.

## Detective Work in Heaton's Parks

This is a drawing of the windmill shown on the old map on page 7. Find the remains in the park.

John Buddle tells us that he tried to rescue the trapped miners from the Chance Pit which was 100 yards east of the windmill.

This is what the Chance Pit looked like. Try to find where it would have been.

John Buddle also tells us that the accident happened 150 yards south of the Chance Pit which would be beyond Adam's house. Try to work out where this was.

# Search on the Internet for exciting places to visit

Google Tanfield Railway

Google Woodhorn Museum

Google Beamish Museum

We remember with sadness the young boys who lost their lives in the awful disaster at Heaton Main Colliery on 3rd May 1815

Thomas Dodd aged 7
William Elliot aged 7
William Graham aged 7
John Pratt aged 10
Thomas Todd aged 7
Thomas Watson aged 10

We also remember the 28 older boys the 41 men and the 50 horses who were also killed

However, we must never forget the great achievements of all the men and boys who worked in the coalmines of Heaton. For almost two hundred years these coalmines were amongst the largest and most advanced in the world. Heaton's heritage, like that of the Northumberland and Durham coalfield, is a heritage to celebrate with great pride.